Baby deserves the very best—and with these three lacy layettes, you can be sure that's exactly what you're creating for that special child. Each set of cardigan, blanket, and bonnet or cap is richly textured and knitted of soft, light weight yarn. Choose from Kitten, Garland, and Blossom patterns. The outfit you create will not only be adorable on Baby, it will become a treasured heirloom.

Leisure Arts, Inc.
Little Rock, Arkansas

Blossom baby set

■■■□ INTERMEDIATE

Shown on front cover and page 14.

Finished Sizes:
Blanket - 34" x 38" (86.5 cm x 96.5 cm)
Bonnet - Size: 3-6 months{9-12 months}
Cardigan - Size: 3{6-12} months
Finished Chest Measurement:
$18^1/_2${$20^1/_4$-$21^3/_4$}"/47{51.5-55} cm

Size Note: Instructions are written for the smallest size with additional size(s) in braces { }. Instructions will be easier to read if you circle all the numbers pertaining to your child's size. If only one number is given, it applies to all sizes.

MATERIALS
LIGHT 3

Light Weight Yarn
[6 ounces, 490 yards
(170 grams, 448 meters) per skein]:
Entire Set - 3 skeins
Blanket - 2 skeins
Bonnet - 1 skein
Cardigan - 1 skein
29" (73.5 cm) Circular knitting needle,
size 7 (4.5 mm) **or** size needed for gauge
Straight knitting needles, size 7 (4.5 mm)
or size needed for gauge (For Cardigan
and Bonnet)
Straight knitting needles, size 5 (3.75 mm)
(For Cardigan Only)
Double pointed knitting needles,
size 7 (4.5 mm) (For Bonnet Only)
Crochet hook, size G (4 mm)
Stitch holders - 3 (For Cardigan Only)
Markers
Point protectors - 2
Yarn needle

GAUGE: With larger size needles,
in Stockinette Stitch,
20 sts and 28 rows = 4" (10 cm)

When instructed to slip a stitch, always slip as if to **knit**.

When you reach a marker, always slip the marker **before** working the following YO.

BLANKET · · · · · · · · · · · · · ·
BOTTOM BAND
Using circular needle, cast on 173 sts.

Rows 1-4: Knit across.

Row 5 (Right side)**:** K3, YO *(Fig. 6a, page 24)*, K2, [slip 1, K2 tog, PSSO *(Figs. 2a & b, page 22)*], K2, ★ YO, K1, YO, K2, slip 1, K2 tog, PSSO, K2; repeat from ★ across to last 3 sts, YO, K3.

Row 6: K2, purl across to last 2 sts, K2.

Rows 7-9: Repeat Rows 5 and 6 once, then repeat Row 5 once **more**.

Rows 10-12: Knit across.

Rows 13-20: Repeat Rows 5-12.

CENTER
Row 1: K3, YO, K2, slip 1, K2 tog, PSSO, K2, YO, place marker *(see Markers, page 22)*, knit across to last 10 sts, place marker, YO, K2, slip 1, K2 tog, PSSO, K2, YO, K3.

Row 2: K2, purl across to last 2 sts, K2.

Row 3: K3, YO, K2, slip 1, K2 tog, PSSO, K2, YO, K3, K2 tog *(Fig. 1, page 22)*, (YO, K6, K2 tog) across to within 4 sts of marker, YO, K4, YO, K2, slip 1, K2 tog, PSSO, K2, YO, K3.

Row 4: K2, purl across to last 2 sts, K2.

Row 5: K3, YO, K2, slip 1, K2 tog, PSSO, K2, YO, K3, YO, slip 1, K2 tog, PSSO, ★ YO, K5, YO, slip 1, K2 tog, PSSO; repeat from ★ across to within 3 sts of marker, YO, K3, YO, K2, slip 1, K2 tog, PSSO, K2, YO, K3.

Row 6: Knit to marker, purl to marker, knit across.

Row 7: K3, YO, K2, slip 1, K2 tog, PSSO, K2, YO, knit to marker, YO, K2, slip 1, K2 tog, PSSO, K2, YO, K3.

Row 8: K2, purl across to last 2 sts, K2.

Row 9: K3, YO, K2, slip 1, K2 tog, PSSO, K2, YO, K8, YO, SSK *(Figs. 3a-c, page 23)*, (K6, YO, SSK) across to within 7 sts of marker, K7, YO, K2, slip 1, K2 tog, PSSO, K2, YO, K3.

Row 10: K2, purl across to last 2 sts, K2.

Row 11: K3, YO, K2, slip 1, K2 tog, PSSO, K2, YO, K7, YO, slip 1, K2 tog, PSSO, ★ YO, K5, YO, slip 1, K2 tog, PSSO; repeat from ★ across to within 7 sts of marker, YO, K7, YO, K2, slip 1, K2 tog, PSSO, K2, YO, K3.

Row 12: Knit to marker, purl to marker, knit across.

Row 13: K3, YO, K2, slip 1, K2 tog, PSSO, K2, YO, knit to marker, YO, K2, slip 1, K2 tog, PSSO, K2, YO, K3.

Repeat Rows 2-13 for pattern until Blanket measures approximately 35" (89 cm) from cast on edge, ending by working Row 7 and removing markers.

TOP BAND

Rows 1-3: Knit across.

Row 4: K3, YO, K2, slip 1, K2 tog, PSSO, K2, ★ YO, K1, YO, K2, slip 1, K2 tog, PSSO, K2; repeat from ★ across to last 3 sts, YO, K3.

Row 5: K2, purl across to last 2 sts, K2.

Rows 6-8: Repeat Rows 4 and 5 once, then repeat Row 4 once **more**.

Rows 9-11: Knit across.

Rows 12-19: Repeat Rows 4-11.

Row 20: K3, M1 *(Figs. 7a & b, page 25)*, K2, slip 1, K2 tog, PSSO, K2, M1, ★ K1, M1, K2, slip 1, K2 tog, PSSO, K2, M1; repeat from ★ across to last 3 sts, K3.

Bind Off Row: K2 tog, ★ slip st back onto left needle, K2 tog; repeat from ★ across, cut yarn and pull through last st.

BONNET • • • • • • • • • • • • • •
BODY
Cast on 61{69} sts.

Rows 1-4: Knit across.

Row 5 (Right side)**:** K3, YO *(Fig. 6a, page 24)*, K2, [slip 1, K2 tog, PSSO *(Figs. 2a & b, page 22)*], K2, ★ YO, K1, YO, K2, slip 1, K2 tog, PSSO, K2; repeat from ★ across to last 3 sts, YO, K3.

Row 6: K2, purl across to last 2 sts, K2.

Rows 7-9: Repeat Rows 5 and 6 once, then repeat Row 5 once **more**.

Instructions continued on page 4.

Rows 10-12: Knit across.

Rows 13-20: Repeat Rows 5-12.

Row 21: K3, YO, K2, slip 1, K2 tog, PSSO, K2, YO, place marker *(see Markers, page 22)*, knit across to last 10 sts, place marker, YO, K2, slip 1, K2 tog, PSSO, K2, YO, K3.

Row 22: K2, purl across to last 2 sts, K2.

Row 23: K3, YO, K2, slip 1, K2 tog, PSSO, K2, YO, K3, K2 tog *(Fig. 1, page 22)*, (YO, K6, K2 tog) across to within 4 sts of marker, YO, K4, YO, K2, slip 1, K2 tog, PSSO, K2, YO, K3.

Row 24: K2, purl across to last 2 sts, K2.

Row 25: K3, YO, K2, slip 1, K2 tog, PSSO, K2, YO, K3, YO, slip 1, K2 tog, PSSO, ★ YO, K5, YO, slip 1, K2 tog, PSSO; repeat from ★ across to within 3 sts of marker, YO, K3, YO, K2, slip 1, K2 tog, PSSO, K2, YO, K3.

Row 26: Knit to marker, purl to marker, knit across.

Row 27: K3, YO, K2, slip 1, K2 tog, PSSO, K2, YO, knit to marker, YO, K2, slip 1, K2 tog, PSSO, K2, YO, K3.

Row 28: K2, purl across to last 2 sts, K2.

Row 29: K3, YO, K2, slip 1, K2 tog, PSSO, K2, YO, K8, YO, SSK *(Figs. 3a-c, page 23)*, (K6, YO, SSK) across to within 7 sts of marker, K7, YO, K2, slip 1, K2 tog, PSSO, K2, YO, K3.

Row 30: K2, purl across to last 2 sts, K2.

Row 31: K3, YO, K2, slip 1, K2 tog, PSSO, K2, YO, K7, YO, slip 1, K2 tog, PSSO, ★ YO, K5, YO, slip 1, K2 tog, PSSO; repeat from ★ across to within 7 sts of marker, YO, K7, YO, K2, slip 1, K2 tog, PSSO, K2, YO, K3.

Row 32: Knit to marker, purl to marker, knit across.

Size Large ONLY
Row 33: K3, YO, K2, slip 1, K2 tog, PSSO, K2, YO, knit to marker, YO, K2, slip 1, K2 tog, PSSO, K2, YO, K3.

Rows 34-38: Repeat Rows 22-26.

BACK
Row 1: Bind off 25{27} sts, knit across: 36{42} sts.

Row 2: Bind off 25{27} sts, purl across: 11{15} sts.

Row 3 (Increase row)**:** K1, M1 *(Figs. 7a & b, page 25)*, knit across to last st, M1, K1: 13{17} sts.

Row 4: Purl across.

Rows 5-8: Repeat Rows 3 and 4 twice: 17{21} sts

Work in Stockinette Stitch until Back measures approximately $3^1/_2${4}"/9{10} cm from bound off edges, ending by working a **purl** row.

Next Row: K2{3}, K2 tog twice, K5{7}, K2 tog twice, K2{3}: 13{17} sts.

Next 3 Rows: Knit across.

Bind off all sts in **knit**.

Sew end of rows of Back to bound off edges of Body.

TIE (Make 2)
Using double pointed needles, cast on 5 sts.

Row 1: P5.

Row 2: K5.

Row 3: P5.

Row 4: K1, slip 1, K2 tog, PSSO, K1: 3 sts.

Row 5: P3.

Row 6: K3.

Row 7: Do **not** turn work; slide 3 sts to opposite end of the needle, K3.

Repeat Row 7 until Tie measures approximately 10" (25.5 cm).

Bind off all sts in **knit**.

Sew cast on edge of Ties to end of rows of Body, $^1/_2$" (12 mm) in from cast on edge.

CARDIGAN

BODY
Using circular needle, cast on 93{101-109} sts.

Rows 1-4: Knit across.

Row 5 (Right side)**:** K3, YO *(Fig. 6a, page 24)*, K2, [slip 1, K2 tog, PSSO *(Figs. 2a & b, page 22)*], K2, ★ YO, K1, YO, K2, slip 1, K2 tog, PSSO, K2; repeat from ★ across to last 3 sts, YO, K3.

Row 6: K2, purl across to last 2 sts, K2.

Rows 7-9: Repeat Rows 5 and 6 once, then repeat Row 5 once **more**.

Rows 10-12: Knit across.

Row 13: K3, YO, K2, slip 1, K2 tog, PSSO, K2, YO, place marker *(see Markers, page 22)*, knit across to last 10 sts, place marker, YO, K2, slip 1, K2 tog, PSSO, K2, YO, K3.

Row 14: K2, purl across to last 2 sts, K2.

Row 15: K3, YO, K2, slip 1, K2 tog, PSSO, K2, YO, knit to marker, YO, K2, slip 1, K2 tog, PSSO, K2, YO, K3.

Row 16: K2, purl across to last 2 sts, K2.

Row 17: K3, YO, K2, slip 1, K2 tog, PSSO, K2, YO, knit to marker, YO, K2, slip 1, K2 tog, PSSO, K2, YO, K3.

Row 18: Knit to marker, purl to marker, knit across.

Row 19: K3, YO, K2, slip 1, K2 tog, PSSO, K2, YO, knit to marker, YO, K2, slip 1, K2 tog, PSSO, K2, YO, K3.

Repeat Rows 14-19 for pattern until Body measures approximately $3^3/_4${$4^3/_4$-$5^1/_4$}"/ 9.5{12-13.5} cm from cast on edge, ending by working a **wrong** side row.

Maintain established pattern throughout.

Dividing Row: Removing markers, work across 21{23-25} sts, slip 21{23-25} sts just worked onto st holder for Right Front, bind off next 4 sts for armhole, K 42{46-50} sts, slip 43{47-51} sts just worked onto second st holder for Back, bind off next 4 sts for armhole, work across: 21{23-25} sts.

LEFT FRONT
Work even until Left Front measures approximately $5^3/_4${$6^3/_4$-$7^1/_2$}"/14.5{17-19} cm from cast on edge, ending by working a **right** side row.

NECK SHAPING
Row 1: Bind off 9 sts, purl across: 12{14-16} sts.

Row 2 (Decrease row)**:** Knit across to last 3 sts, K2 tog *(Fig. 1, page 22)*, K1: 11{13-15} sts.

Row 3: P1, P2 tog *(Fig. 4, page 23)*, purl across: 10{12-14} sts.

Instructions continued on page 6.

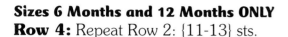

Sizes 6 Months and 12 Months ONLY
Row 4: Repeat Row 2: {11-13} sts.

All Sizes
Work even until Left Front measures approximately 8{9-9³/₄}"/20.5{23-25} cm from cast on edge, ending by working a **purl** row.

Slip remaining sts onto st holder; cut yarn.

RIGHT FRONT
With **wrong** side facing, slip 21{23-25} sts from Right Front st holder onto larger size needle.

Beginning with a **wrong** side row, work even until Right Front measures approximately 5³/₄{6³/₄-7¹/₂}"/14.5{17-19} cm from cast on edge, ending by working a **wrong** side row.

NECK SHAPING
Row 1: Bind off 9 sts, knit across: 12{14-16} sts.

Row 2 (Decrease row)**:** Purl across to last 3 sts, P2 tog tbl *(Fig. 5, page 23)*, P1: 11{13-15} sts.

Row 3: K1, SSK *(Figs. 3a-c, page 23)*, knit across: 10{12-14} sts.

Sizes 6 Months and 12 Months ONLY
Row 4: Repeat Row 2: {11-13} sts.

All Sizes
Work even until Right Front measures same as Left Front, ending by working a **knit** row.

Slip remaining sts onto st holder; cut yarn leaving a long end for 3-needle bind off.

BACK
With **wrong** side facing, slip 43{47-51} sts from Back st holder onto circular needle.

Beginning with a **purl** row, work in Stockinette Stitch until Back measures same as Fronts to shoulder, ending by working a **knit** row.

Leave remaining sts on circular needle; do **not** cut yarn.

SHOULDER JOININGS
Slip sts from Left Front st holder onto straight needle. Using 3-needle bind off method *(Fig. 8, page 25)*, join first 10{11-13} sts of Back to Left Front.

Slip sts from Right Front st holder onto straight needle. Using long end from Right Front and 3-needle bind off method, join Right Front to Back.

Leave remaining Back sts on circular needle. Place point protectors on each end of circular needle to prevent sts from falling off.

SLEEVE (Make 2)
Using larger size straight needles, cast on 29{29-37} sts.

Rows 1-4: Knit across.

Row 5 (Right side)**:** K3, YO, K2, slip 1, K2 tog, PSSO, K2, ★ YO, K1, YO, K2, slip 1, K2 tog, PSSO, K2; repeat from ★ across to last 3 sts, YO, K3.

Row 6: Purl across.

Rows 7-9: Repeat Rows 5 and 6 once, then repeat Row 5 once **more**.

Rows 10-12: Knit across.

Row 13: K6{6-2}, M1 *(Figs. 7a & b, page 25)*, ★ K1{1-3}, M1; repeat from ★ across to last 6{6-2} sts, K6{6-2}: 47{47-49} sts.

Row 14 AND ALL WRONG SIDE ROWS: Purl across.

Row 15: Knit across.

Row 17: K6{6-7}, K2 tog, (YO, K6, K2 tog) across to last 7{7-8} sts, YO, K7{7-8}.

Row 19: K6{6-7}, YO, slip 1, K2 tog, PSSO, ★ YO, K5, YO, slip 1, K2 tog, PSSO; repeat from ★ across to last 6{6-7} sts, YO, K6{6-7}.

Row 21: Knit across.

Row 23: K3{3-4}, YO, SSK, (K6, YO, SSK) across to last 2{2-3} sts, K2{2-3}.

Row 25: K2{2-3}, YO, slip 1, K2 tog, PSSO, ★ YO, K5, YO, slip 1, K2 tog, PSSO; repeat from ★ across to last 2{2-3} sts, YO, K2{2-3}.

Repeat Rows 14-25 for pattern until Sleeve measures approximately 6¹/₂{7-8}"/16.5{18-20.5} cm from cast on edge, ending by working Row 16 or Row 22.

Bind off all sts in **knit**.

FINISHING
Matching center of last row of Sleeve to shoulder joining, sew top of Sleeve to edge of Body being careful not to catch armhole bound off sts.

Sew Sleeve edges to armhole bound off sts and weave Sleeve seams *(Fig. 10, page 26)*.

NECKBAND
With **right** side facing and smaller size needles, pick up 17{19-21} sts along Right Front neck edge *(Figs. 9a & b, page 25)*, K 23{25-25} from circular needle, pick up 17{19-21} sts along Left Front neck edge: 57{63-67} sts.

Rows 1-5: Knit across.

Bind off all sts in **knit**.

TIES
Refer to Basic Crochet Stitches, page 26.

With **right** side facing and using crochet hook, join yarn with slip st along Front edge below Neckband; chain a 6" (15 cm) length; finish off.

Repeat for second side.

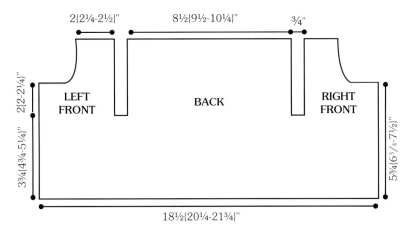

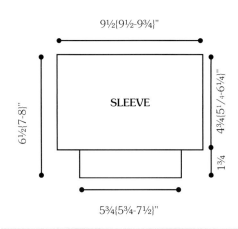

Sleeve width includes two edge stitches.

Garland baby set

Shown on pages 1 and 28.

Finished Sizes:

Blanket - 35" (89 cm) square
Cap - Size: 3-6 months{9-12 months}
Finished Measurement:
12{13¹/₄}"/30.5{33.5} cm
Cardigan - Size: 3{6-12} months
Finished Chest Measurement:
19{20¹/₂-22}"/48.5{52-56} cm

Size Note: Instructions are written for the smallest size with additional size(s) in braces { }. Instructions will be easier to read if you circle all the numbers pertaining to your child's size. If only one number is given, it applies to all sizes.

MATERIALS

Light Weight Yarn 🧶 **3** LIGHT
[7 ounces, 575 yards
(198 grams, 525 meters) per skein]:
Entire Set - 3 skeins
Blanket - 2 skeins
Cap - 1 skein
Cardigan - 1 skein
29" (73.5 cm) Circular knitting needle,
size 6 (4 mm) **or** size needed for gauge
Straight knitting needles, size 6 (4 mm)
or size needed for gauge (For Cardigan
and Cap)
Straight knitting needles, size 4 (3.5 mm)
(For Cardigan only)
Stitch holders - 4 (For Cardigan Only)
Markers
Point protectors - 2
Yarn needle
⁹/₁₆" (14 mm) Buttons - 2 (For Cardigan Only)

GAUGE: With larger size needles,
in Stockinette Stitch,
22 sts and 30 rows = 4" (10 cm)

When instructed to slip a stitch, always slip as if to **knit**.

Always slip marker **after** working the YO.

BLANKET • • • • • • • • • • • •
BOTTOM EDGING
Using circular needle, cast on 169 sts.

Rows 1-19: Knit across.

Row 20 (Right side)**:** K 12, place marker *(see Markers, page 22)*, knit across to last 12 sts, place marker, knit across.

Row 21: Knit to marker, purl to marker, knit across.

Row 22: Knit to marker, K1, [YO *(Fig. 6a, page 24)*, K2 tog *(Fig. 1, page 22)*] across to marker, knit across.

Row 23: Knit to marker, purl to marker, knit across.

Rows 24-26: Knit across.

BOTTOM BAND

Row 1: Knit to marker, purl to marker, knit across.

Row 2: Knit to marker, K3, YO, **[**slip 1, K2 tog, PSSO *(Figs. 2a & b, page 22)***]**, ★ YO, K5, YO, slip 1, K2 tog, PSSO; repeat from ★ across to within 3 sts of marker, YO, knit across.

Row 3: Knit to marker, purl to marker, knit across.

Row 4: Knit to marker, K1, K2 tog, YO, K3, YO, SSK *(Figs. 3a-c, page 23)*, K1, ★ K2 tog, YO, K3, YO, SSK, K1; repeat from ★ across to marker, knit across.

Repeat Rows 1-4 for pattern until Blanket measures approximately 9¼" (23.5 cm) from cast on edge, ending by working Row 3.

CENTER
Row 1: Knit to marker, K1, (K2 tog, YO, K3, YO, SSK, K1) 4 times, place marker, K7, **[**M1 *(Figs. 7a & b, page 25)*, K8**]** 9 times, place marker, (K1, K2 tog, YO, K3, YO, SSK) 4 times, knit across: 178 sts.

Row 2: Knit to marker, purl to last marker, knit across.

Row 3: ★ Knit to marker, K3, YO, slip 1, K2 tog, PSSO, YO, (K5, YO, slip 1, K2 tog, PSSO, YO) 3 times, K3; repeat from ★ once **more**, knit across.

Row 4: Knit to marker, purl to last marker, knit across.

Row 5: ★ Knit to marker, K1, (K2 tog, YO, K3, YO, SSK, K1) 4 times; repeat from ★ once **more**, knit across.

Repeat Rows 2-5 for pattern until Blanket measures approximately 25¾" (65.5 cm) from cast on edge, ending by working Row 4.

TOP BAND
Row 1: Knit to marker, K1, (K2 tog, YO, K3, YO, SSK, K1) 4 times, remove marker, K7, (K2 tog, K7) 9 times, remove marker, (K1, K2 tog, YO, K3, YO, SSK) 4 times, knit across: 169 sts.

Row 2: Knit to marker, purl to marker, knit across.

Row 3: Knit to marker, K3, YO, slip 1, K2 tog, PSSO, ★ YO, K5, YO, slip 1, K2 tog, PSSO; repeat from ★ across to within 3 sts of marker, YO, knit across.

Row 4: Knit to marker, purl to marker, knit across.

Row 5: Knit to marker, K1, ★ K2 tog, YO, K3, YO, SSK, K1; repeat from ★ across to marker, knit across.

Repeat Rows 2-5 for pattern until Blanket measures approximately 32½" (82.5 cm) from cast on edge, ending by working a **wrong** side row.

TOP EDGING
Rows 1-3: Knit across.

Row 4: Knit to marker, purl to marker, knit across.

Row 5: Knit to marker, K1, (YO, K2 tog) across to marker, knit across.

Row 6: Knit to marker, purl to marker, knit across.

Rows 7-24: Knit across.

Bind off all sts in **knit**.

CAP • • • • • • • • • • • • • • •
BODY
Using larger size straight needles, cast on 65{73} sts.

Rows 1-6: Knit across.

Instructions continued on page 10.

Row 7: Purl across.

Row 8 (Right side)**:** K2, **[**YO *(Fig. 6a, page 24)*, K2 tog *(Fig. 1, page 22)***]** across to last st, K1.

Row 9: Purl across.

Rows 10 and 11: Knit across.

Row 12: Knit across to last st, M1 *(Figs. 7a & b, page 25)*, K1: 66{74} sts.

Row 13: Purl across.

Row 14: K3, YO, **[**slip 1, K2 tog, PSSO *(Figs. 2a & b, page 22)***]**, ★ YO, K5, YO, slip 1, K2 tog, PSSO; repeat from ★ across to last 4 sts, YO, K4.

Row 15: Purl across.

Row 16: ★ K1, K2 tog, YO, K3, YO, SSK *(Figs. 3a-c, page 23)*; repeat from ★ across to last 2 sts, K2.

Repeat Rows 13-16 for pattern until Body measures approximately 4^1/$_2$}{5}"/11.5{12.5} cm from cast on edge, ending by working a **purl** row.

CROWN
Row 1: ★ K1, K2 tog, K3, SSK; repeat from ★ across to last 2 sts, K2: 50{56} sts.

Row 2 AND ALL WRONG SIDE ROWS THROUGH ROW 10: Purl across.

Row 3: Knit across.

Row 5: K2, ★ slip 1, K2 tog, PSSO, K3; repeat from ★ across: 34{38} sts.

Row 7: Knit across.

Row 9: ★ K1, slip 1, K2 tog, PSSO; repeat from ★ across to last 2 sts, K2: 18{20} sts.

Row 11: K2 tog across; cut yarn leaving a long end for sewing: 9{10} sts.

Thread needle with long end and weave through remaining sts on Row 11, gather tightly; with same yarn, weave seam *(Fig. 10, page 26)*.

CARDIGAN · · · · · · · · · · ·
BODY
Using circular needle, cast on 107{115-123} sts.

Rows 1-5: Knit across.

Row 6 (Right side)**:** K5, place marker *(see Markers, page 22)*, knit across to last 5 sts, place marker, K5.

Row 7: Knit to marker, purl to marker, knit across.

Row 8: Knit to marker, K1, **[**YO *(Fig. 6a, page 24)*, K2 tog *(Fig. 1, page 22)***]** across to marker, knit across.

Row 9: Knit to marker, purl to marker, knit across.

Rows 10-12: Knit across.

Row 13: Knit to marker, purl to marker, knit across.

Row 14: Knit to marker, K3, YO, **[**slip 1, K2 tog, PSSO *(Figs. 2a & b, page 22)***]**, ★ YO, K5, YO, slip 1, K2 tog, PSSO; repeat from ★ across within 3 sts of marker, YO, knit across.

Row 15: Knit to marker, purl to marker, knit across.

Row 16: Knit to marker, K1, ★ K2 tog, YO, K3, YO, SSK *(Figs. 3a-c, page 23)*, K1; repeat from ★ across to marker, knit across.

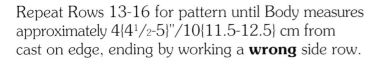

Repeat Rows 13-16 for pattern until Body measures approximately 4{4$^1/_2$-5}"/10{11.5-12.5} cm from cast on edge, ending by working a **wrong** side row.

Dividing Row: Removong markers, K 27{28-29}, slip 27{28-29} sts just worked onto st holder for Right Front, bind off next 4{6-8} sts for armhole, K 44{46-48}, slip 45{47-49} sts just worked onto second st holder for Back, bind off next 4{6-8} sts for armhole, knit across: 27{28-29} sts.

LEFT FRONT
Row 1: K5, purl across.

Row 2: Knit across.

Repeat Rows 1 and 2 for pattern until Left Front measures approximately 5$^3/_4${6$^1/_4$-7}"/ 14.5{16-18} cm from cast on edge, ending by working a **right** side row.

NECK SHAPING
Row 1: K5, P6, slip 11 sts just worked onto st holder, purl across: 16{17-18} sts.

Row 2 (Decrease row)**:** Knit across to last 3 sts, K2 tog, K1: 15{16-17} sts.

Row 3 (Decrease row)**:** P1, P2 tog *(Fig. 4, page 23)*, purl across: 14{15-16} sts.

Continue to decrease one stitch at neck edge, every row, 4{4-5} times **more**: 10{11-11} sts.

Work even until Left Front measures approximately 8$^1/_4${8$^3/_4$-10}"/21{22-25.5} cm from cast on edge, ending by working a **purl** row; cut yarn.

Slip remaining sts onto st holder.

RIGHT FRONT
With **wrong** side facing, slip 27{28-29} sts from Right Front st holder onto larger size needle.

Row 1: Purl across to last 5 sts, K5.

Row 2: Knit across.

Row 3: Purl across to last 5 sts, K5.

Size 12 months ONLY
Rows 4 and 5: Repeat Rows 2 and 3.

All Sizes
Row 4{4-6} (Buttonhole row)**:** K1, **[**K2 tog, YO (buttonhole)**]**, knit across.

Rows 5{5-7} thru 11{11-13}: Repeat Rows 1 and 2, 3 times; then repeat Row 1 once **more**.

Row 12{12-14}: Repeat Row 4{4-6}.

Work even until Right Front measures approximately 5$^3/_4${6$^1/_4$-7}"/14.5{16-18} cm from cast on edge, ending by working a **right** side row.

NECK SHAPING
Row 1: P 16{17-18}, slip last 11 sts onto st holder: 16{17-18} sts.

Row 2 (Decrease row)**:** K1, SSK, knit across: 15{16-17} sts.

Row 3 (Decrease row)**:** Purl across to last 3 sts, P2 tog tbl *(Fig. 5, page 23)*: 14{15-16} sts.

Continue to decrease one stitch at neck edge, every row, 4{4-5} times **more**: 10{11-11} sts.

Instructions continued on page 12.

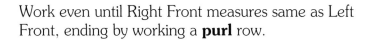

Work even until Right Front measures same as Left Front, ending by working a **purl** row.

Slip remaining sts onto st holder; cut yarn leaving a long end for 3-needle bind off.

BACK

With **wrong** side facing, slip 45{47-49} sts from Back st holder onto circular needle.

Beginning with a **purl** row, work in Stockinette Stitch until Back measures same as Fronts, ending by working a **knit** row.

Leave remaining sts on circular needle; do **not** cut yarn.

SHOULDER JOININGS

Slip sts from Left Front shoulder st holder onto larger size straight needle. Using 3-needle bind off method *(Fig. 8, page 25)*, join first 10{11-11} sts of Back to Left Front.

Slip sts from Right Front shoulder st holder onto larger size straight needle. Using long end from Right Front and 3-needle bind off method, join Right Front to Back.

Leave remaining 25{ 25-27} sts of Back on circular needle. Place point protectors on each end of circular needle to prevent sts from falling off.

SLEEVE (Make 2)

Using larger size straight needles, cast on 31{31-33} sts.

Rows 1-6: Knit across.

Row 7: Purl across.

Row 8: (Right side): K2, (YO, K2 tog) across to last st, K1.

Row 9: Purl across.

Rows 10 and 11: Knit across.

Row 12: K1, M1 *(Figs. 7a & b, page 25)*, K 10, M1, K9{9-11}, M1, K 10, M1, K1: 35{35-37} sts.

Rows 13-15: Beginning with a **purl** row, work in Stockinette Stitch.

Row 16 (Increase row): K1, M1, knit across to last st, M1, K1: 37{37-39} sts.

Continue to increase one stitch in same manner at each edge, every fourth row, 8{8-6} times **more**; then increase every sixth row, 0{0-3} times *(see Zeros, page 22)*: 53{53-57} sts.

Work even until Sleeve measures approximately 6³/₄{7¹/₄-8¹/₂}"/17{18.5-21.5} cm from cast on edge, ending by working a **purl** row.

Bind off all sts in **knit**.

FINISHING

Matching center of last row of Sleeve to shoulder joining, sew top of Sleeve to edge of Body being careful not to catch armhole bound off sts.

Sew Sleeve edges to armhole bound off sts and weave Sleeve seams *(Fig. 10, page 26)*.

NECKBAND

With **right** side facing and smaller size needles, knit 11 sts from Right Front st holder, pick up 11{11-13} sts evenly spaced along Right Front neck edge *(Fig. 9a, page 25)*, knit 25{25-27} sts from circular needle, pick up 11{11-13} sts evenly spaced along Left Front neck edge, slip 11 sts from Left Front st holder onto empty needle and knit across: 69{69-75} sts.

Rows 1-4: Knit across.

Bind off all sts **knit**.

Sew buttons to Left Front opposite buttonholes.

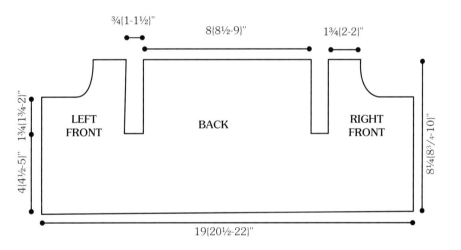

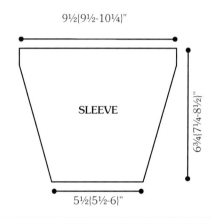

Sleeve width includes two edge stitches.

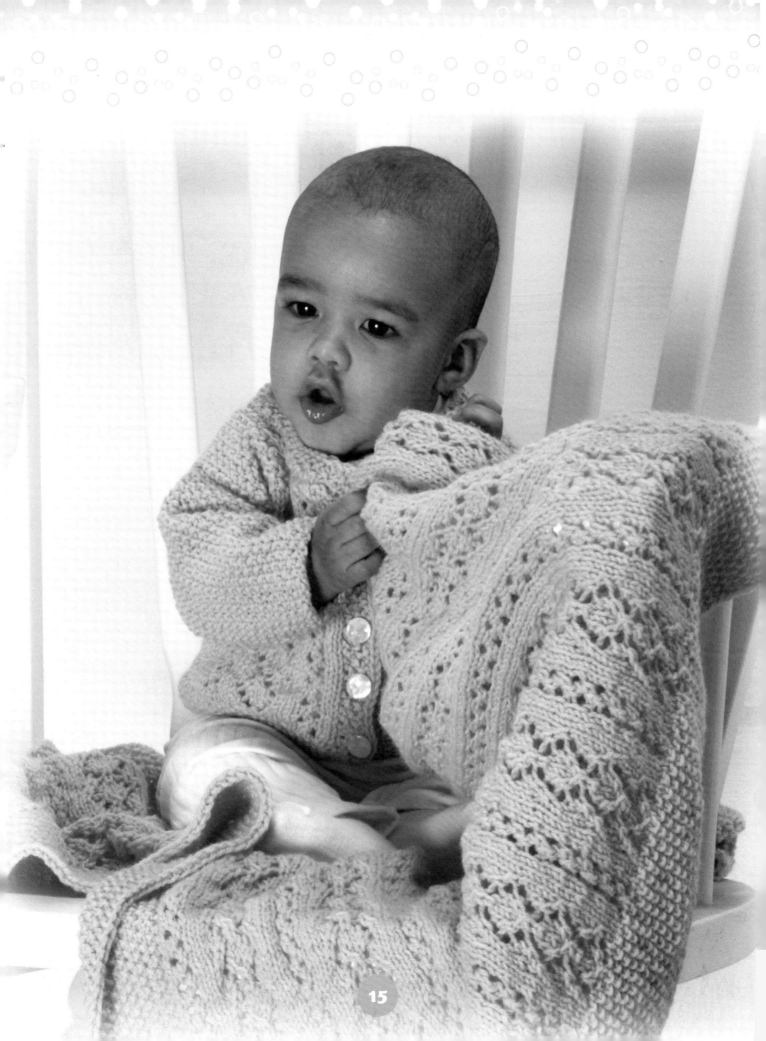

Kitten baby set

Shown on back cover and page 15.

Finished Sizes:
Blanket - 36" (91.5 cm) square
Bonnet - Size: 3{6-12} months
Cardigan - Size: 3{6-12} months
Finished Measurement:
18³/₄{20¹/₂-22}"/47.5{52-56} cm

Size Note: Instructions are written for size 3 months with sizes 6 months and 12 months in braces { }. Instructions will be easier to read if you circle all the numbers pertaining to your child's size. If only one number is given, it applies to all sizes.

MATERIALS
Light Weight Yarn ③ LIGHT
[5 ounces, 459 yards
(140 grams, 420 meters) per skein]:
    Entire Set - 4 skeins
    Blanket - 3 skeins
    Bonnet - 1 skein
    Cardigan - 1 skein
29" (73.5 cm) Circular knitting needle,
    size 7 (4.5 mm) **or** size needed for gauge
Straight knitting needles, size 7 (4.5 mm)
    or size needed for gauge
    (For Cardigan and Bonnet)
Straight knitting needles, size 5 (3.75 mm)
    (For Cardigan Only)
Stitch holders - 3 (For Cardigan Only)
Markers
Point protectors - 2
Yarn needle
⁹/₁₆" (14 mm) Buttons - 4{5-5}
    (For Cardigan Only)

GAUGE:
With larger size needles,
in Seed Stitch,
20 sts and 35 rows = 4" (10 cm)
in Stockinette Stitch,
20 sts and 28 rows = 4" (10 cm)

When instructed to slip a stitch, always slip as if to **knit**, unless instructed otherwise.

BLANKET • • • • • • • • • • •
BOTTOM BAND
Using circular needle, cast on 177 sts.

Row 1: (K1, P1) across to last st, WYF slip 1 as if to **purl**.

Repeat Row 1 (Seed St) until Blanket measures approximately 3" (7.5 cm) from cast on edge.

CENTER
Row 1 (Right side)**:** K1, (P1, K1) 7 times, place marker **(see Markers, page 22)**, K1, YO **(Fig. 6a, page 24)**, K2 tog **(Fig. 1, page 22)**, ★ K3, K2 tog, YO, K1, YO, SSK **(Figs. 3a-c, page 23)**, K3, YO, K2 tog; repeat from ★ 10 times **more**, K1, place marker, (K1, P1) across to last st, WYF slip 1 as if to **purl**.

Row 2 AND ALL WRONG SIDE ROWS THROUGHOUT CENTER: K1, (P1, K1) to marker, purl to marker, (K1, P1) across to last st, WYF slip 1 as if to **purl**.

Row 3: K1, (P1, K1) to marker, K1, SSK, ★ YO, K2, K2 tog, YO, K3, YO, SSK, K2, SSK; repeat from ★ across to within one st of marker, YO, K2, P1, (K1, P1) across to last st, WYF slip 1 as if to **purl**.

Row 5: K1, (P1, K1) to marker, K1, YO, K2 tog, ★ K3, YO, SSK, K1, K2 tog, YO, K3, YO, K2 tog; repeat from ★ across to within one st of marker, K2, P1, (K1, P1) across to last st, WYF slip 1 as if to **purl**.

Row 7: K1, (P1, K1) to marker, K1, SSK, ★ YO, K4, YO, [slip 1, K2 tog, PSSO *(Figs. 2a & b, page 22)*], YO, K4, SSK; repeat from ★ across to within one st of marker, YO, K2, P1, (K1, P1) across to last st, WYF slip 1 as if to **purl**.

Row 9: K1, (P1, K1) to marker, K1, YO, K2 tog, ★ K3, K2 tog, YO, K1, YO, SSK, K3, YO, K2 tog; repeat from ★ across to within one st of marker, K2, P1, (K1, P1) across to last st, WYF slip 1 as if to **purl**.

Repeat Rows 2-9 for pattern until Blanket measures approximately 33" (84 cm) from cast on edge, ending by working Row 8 and removing markers on last row.

TOP BAND
Row 1: (K1, P1) across to last st, WYF slip 1 as if to **purl**.

Repeat Row 1 until Blanket measures approximately 36" (91.5 cm) from cast on edge.

Bind off all sts in pattern.

BONNET • • • • • • • • • • • •
FRONT BAND
Using larger size needles, cast on 53{57-65} sts.

Rows 1 thru 9{13-19}: (K1, P1) across to last st, WYF slip 1 as if to **purl**.

BODY
Row 1 (Right side)**:** K1, (P1, K1) 2{3-5} times, place marker *(see Markers, page 22)*, K1, YO *(Fig. 6a, page 24)*, K2 tog *(Fig. 1, page 22)*, ★ K3, K2 tog, YO, K1, YO, SSK *(Figs. 3a-c, page 23)*, K3, YO, K2 tog; repeat from ★ 2 times **more**, K1, place marker, (K1, P1) 2{3-5} times, WYF slip 1 as if to **purl**.

Row 2 AND ALL WRONG SIDE ROWS THROUGHOUT BODY: K1, (P1, K1) to marker, purl to marker, (K1, P1) 2{3-5} times, WYF slip 1 as if to **purl**.

Row 3: K1, (P1, K1) to marker, K1, SSK, ★ YO, K2, K2 tog, YO, K3, YO, SSK, K2, SSK; repeat from ★ across to within one st of marker, YO, K2, P1, (K1, P1) 1{2-4} time(s), WYF slip 1 as if to **purl.**

Row 5: K1, (P1, K1) to marker, K1, YO, K2 tog, ★ K3, YO, SSK, K1, K2 tog, YO, K3, YO, K2 tog; repeat from ★ across to within one st of marker, K2, P1, (K1, P1) 1{2-4} time(s), WYF slip 1 as if to **purl**.

Row 7: K1, (P1, K1) to marker, K1, SSK, ★ YO, K4, YO, [slip 1, K2 tog, PSSO *(Figs. 2a & b, page 22)*], YO, K4, SSK; repeat from ★ across to within one st of marker, YO, K2, P1, (K1, P1) 1{2-4} time(s), WYF slip 1 as if to **purl**.

Row 9: K1, (P1, K1) to marker, K1, YO, K2 tog, ★ K3, K2 tog, YO, K1, YO, SSK, K3, YO, K2 tog; repeat from ★ across to within one st of marker, K2, P1, (K1, P1) 1{2-4} time(s), WYF slip 1 as if to **purl**.

Rows 10-24: Repeat Rows 2-9 once, then repeat Rows 2-8 once **more**.

Instructions continued on page 18.

BACK

Row 1: Bind off 20{21-23} sts in **knit**, work across: 33{36-42} sts.

Row 2: Bind off 20{21-23} sts in **purl**, purl across: 13{15-19} sts.

Row 3: (K1, P1) across to last st, WYF slip 1 as if to **purl**.

Repeat Row 3 until Back measures approximately 3³/₄{4-4¹/₂}"/9.5{10-11.5} cm from bound off edges.

Bind off all sts in pattern.

Sew end of rows of Back to bound off edges of Body.

TIE (Make 2)

Using larger size needles, cast on 52{56-60} sts.

Row 1: Knit across.

Bind off all sts in **knit**.

Sew one end of each Tie to end of rows of Front Band.

CARDIGAN

BACK

LOWER BAND

Using smaller size needles, cast on 45{49-53} sts.

Rows 1-9: K1, (P1, K1) across (Seed Stitch).

BODY

Change to larger size circular needle.

Row 1 (Right side)**:** Knit across increasing 4 sts evenly spaced: 49{53-57} sts.

Beginning with a **purl** row, work in Stockinette Stitch until Back measures approximately 8{9-9³/₄}"/20.5{23-25} cm from cast on edge, ending by working a **knit** row.

Leave sts on circular needle. Place point protectors on each end of circular needle to prevent sts from falling off; cut yarn.

LEFT FRONT

LOWER BAND

Using smaller size needles, cast on 23{25-27} sts.

Rows 1-9: K1, (P1, K1) across.

BODY

Change to larger size straight needles.

Row 1 (Right side)**:** K5{7-9}, YO *(Figs. 6a-c, page 24)*, K2 tog *(Fig. 1, page 22)*, K3, K2 tog, YO, K1, YO, SSK *(Figs. 3a-c, page 23)*, K3, YO, K2 tog, K3.

Row 2 AND ALL WRONG SIDE ROWS THROUGH ROW 32{40-40}: Purl across.

Row 3: K5{7-9}, SSK, YO, K2, K2 tog, YO, K3, YO, SSK, K2, SSK, YO, K3.

Row 5: K5{7-9}, YO, K2 tog, K3, YO, SSK, K1, K2 tog, YO, K3, YO, K2 tog, K3.

Row 7: K5{7-9}, SSK, YO, K4, YO, [slip 1, K2 tog, PSSO *(Figs. 2a & b, page 22)*], YO, K4, SSK, YO, K3.

Rows 9-32{40-40}: Repeat Rows 1-8, 3{4-4} times.

Next 1{1-3} Row(s): K1, (P1, K1) across.

NECK SHAPING

Row 1: Bind off 6{7-7} sts, work across in Seed Stitch: 17{18-20} sts.

Row 2 (Decrease row)**:** Work across to last 3 sts, K2 tog, K1: 16{17-19} sts.

Row 3 (Decrease row)**:** P1, P2 tog *(Fig. 4, page 23)*, work across: 15{16-18} sts.

Continue to decrease one st at neck edge every row, 4{5-5} times **more**: 11{11-13} sts.

Work even until Left Front measures same as Back, ending by working a **purl** row; do **not** cut yarn.

Shoulder Joining: Using 3-needle bind off method *(Fig. 8, page 25)*, join first 11{11-13} sts of Left Front to Back. Leave remaining Back sts on circular needle; place point protectors on needle.

RIGHT FRONT
LOWER BAND
Using smaller size needles, cast on 23{25-27} sts.

Rows 1-9: K1, (P1, K1) across.

BODY
Change to larger size straight needles.

Row 1 (Right side)**:** K3, YO, K2 tog, K3, K2 tog, YO, K1, YO, SSK, K3, YO, K2 tog, K5{7-9}.

Row 2 AND ALL WRONG SIDE ROWS THROUGH ROW 32{40-40}: Purl across.

Row 3: K3, SSK, YO, K2, K2 tog, YO, K3, YO, SSK, K2, SSK, YO, K5{7-9}.

Row 5: K3, YO, K2 tog, K3, YO, SSK, K1, K2 tog, YO, K3, YO, K2 tog, K5{7-9}.

Row 7: K3, SSK, YO, K4, YO, slip 1, K2 tog, PSSO, YO, K4, SSK, YO, K5{7-9}.
Rows 9 thru 32{40-40}: Repeat Rows 1-8, 3{4-4} times.

Next 2{2-4} Rows: K1, (P1, K1) across.

NECK SHAPING
Row 1: Bind off 6{7-7} sts, work across: 17{18-20} sts.

Row 2 (Decrease row)**:** Work across to last 3 sts, P2 tog tbl *(Fig. 5, page 23)*, P1: 16{17-19} sts.

Row 3 (Decrease row)**:** K1, SSK, work across: 15{16-18} sts.

Continue to decrease one st at neck edge every row, 4{5-5} times **more**: 11{11-13} sts.

Work even until Right Front measures same as Back, ending by working a **knit** row.

Shoulder Joining: With **right** side facing, slip Back sts to right end of circular needle. Using 3-needle bind off method, join Right Front to first 11{11-13} sts of Back. Leave remaining 27{31-31} sts of Back on circular needle. Place point protectors on needle.

SLEEVE (Make 2)
Using larger size straight needles, cast on 27{29-31} sts.

Rows 1-5: (K1, P1) across to last st, WYF slip 1 as if to **purl**.

Row 6 (Right side - Increase row)**:** K1, M1 *(Figs. 7a & b, page 25)*, P1, (K1, P1) across to last st, M1, WYF slip 1 as if to **purl**: 29{31-33} sts.

Rows 7-11: K2, (P1, K1) across to last st, WYF slip 1 as if to **purl**.

Row 12 (Increase row)**:** K1, M1, K1, (P1, K1) across to last st, M1, WYF slip 1 as if to **purl**: 31{33-35} sts.

Rows 13-17: (K1, P1) across to last st, WYF slip 1 as if to **purl**.

Instructions continued on page 20.

Maintaining pattern, continue to increase one st at each edge, every sixth row, 5{3-4} times **more**, then increase every eighth row, 0{2-2} times **(see Zeros, page 22)**: 41{43-47} sts.

Work even until Sleeve measures approximately 6{6½-7½}"/15{16.5-19} cm from cast on edge, ending by working a **wrong** side row.

Last Row: Purl across.

Bind off all sts in **knit**.

FINISHING
Place a marker through the edge st on Back and Fronts 4{4¼-4½}"/10{11-11.5} cm down from shoulder joining. Matching center of last row of Sleeve to shoulder joining, sew top of Sleeve to edge of Body beginning and ending at markers.

Weave underarm and side in one continuous seam **(Fig. 10, page 26)**.

NECKBAND
With **right** side facing and smaller size needles, pick up 15{17-20} sts along Right Front neck edge **(Figs. 9a & b, page 25)**, K 27{31-31} from circular needle, pick up 15{17-20} sts along Left Front neck edge: 57{65-71} sts.

Rows 1-4: K1, (P1, K1) across.

Bind off all sts in **knit**.

LEFT FRONT BAND
With **right** side facing and smaller size needles, pick up 33{39-41} sts evenly spaced across Left Front edge.

Rows 1-5: (K1, P1) across to last st, WYF slip 1 as if to **purl**.

Bind off all sts in **knit**.

RIGHT FRONT BAND
Work same as Left Front Band through Row 2.

Row 3 (Buttonhole row)**:** (K1, P1) twice, **[**YO, K2 tog (buttonhole)**]**, (work across next 5 sts, YO, K2 tog) 3{4-4} times, work across to last st, WYF slip 1 as if to **purl**.

Rows 4 and 5: (K1, P1) across to last st, WYF slip 1 as if to **purl**.

Bind off all sts in **knit**.

Sew buttons to Left Front Band opposite buttonholes.

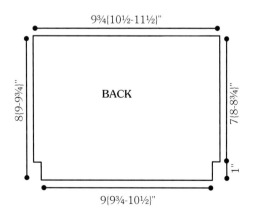

BACK

9¾{10½-11½}"

8{9-9¾}"   7{8-8¾}"

9{9¾-10½}"   1"

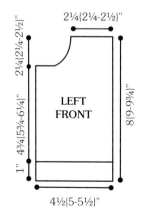

2¼{2¼-2½}"

2¼{2¼-2½}"

4¾{5¾-6¼}"

LEFT FRONT

1"   8{9-9¾}"

4½{5-5½}"

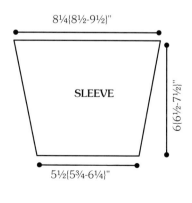

8¼{8½-9½}"

SLEEVE

6{6½-7½}"

5½{5¾-6¼}"

Cardigan dimensions include two edge stitches.

General instructions

ABBREVIATIONS

cm	centimeters
K	knit
M1	make one
mm	millimeters
P	purl
PSSO	pass slipped stitch over
SSK	slip, slip, knit
st(s)	stitch(es)
tbl	through back loop(s)
tog	together
WYF	with yarn in front
YO	yarn over

★ — work instructions following ★ as many **more** times as indicated in addition to the first time.

( ) or [ ] — work enclosed instructions **as many** times as specified by the number immediately following **or** contains explanatory remarks.

colon (:) — the number(s) given after a colon at the end of a row denotes the number of stitches or spaces you should have on that row or round.

work even — work without increasing or decreasing in the established pattern.

GAUGE

Exact gauge is **essential** for proper size or fit. Before beginning your project, make a sample swatch in the yarn and needle specified. After completing the swatch, measure it, counting your stitches and rows carefully. If your swatch is larger or smaller than specified, **make another, changing needle size to get the correct gauge**. Keep trying until you find the size needles that will give you the specified gauge. Once proper gauge is obtained, measure width of garment approximately every 3" (7.5 cm) to be sure gauge remains consistent.

KNIT TERMINOLOGY	
UNITED STATES	INTERNATIONAL
gauge =	tension
bind off =	cast off
yarn over (YO) =	yarn forward (yfwd) **or**
	yarn around needle (yrn)

Yarn Weight Symbol & Names	SUPER FINE 1	FINE 2	LIGHT 3	MEDIUM 4	BULKY 5	SUPER BULKY 6
Type of Yarns in Category	Sock, Fingering Baby	Sport, Baby	DK, Light Worsted	Worsted, Afghan, Aran	Chunky, Craft, Rug	Bulky, Roving
Knit Gauge Ranges in Stockinette St to 4" (10 cm)	27-32 sts	23-26 sts	21-24 sts	16-20 sts	12-15 sts	6-11 sts
Advised Needle Size Range	1-3	3-5	5-7	7-9	9-11	11 and larger

KNITTING NEEDLES															
U.S.	0	1	2	3	4	5	6	7	8	9	10	10½	11	13	15	17
U.K.	13	12	11	10	9	8	7	6	5	4	3	2	1	00	000	---
Metric - mm	2	2.25	2.75	3.25	3.5	3.75	4	4.5	5	5.5	6	6.5	8	9	10	12.75

◼◻◻◻ BEGINNER	Projects for first-time knitters using basic knit and purl stitches. Minimal shaping.
◼◼◻◻ EASY	Projects using basic stitches, repetitive stitch patterns, simple color changes, and simple shaping and finishing.
◼◼◼◻ INTERMEDIATE	Projects with a variety of stitches, such as basic cables and lace, simple intarsia, double-pointed needles and knitting in the round needle techniques, mid-level shaping and finishing.
◼◼◼◼ EXPERIENCED	Projects using advanced techniques and stitches, such as short rows, fair isle, more intricate intarsia, cables, lace patterns, and numerous color changes.

ZEROS

To consolidate the length of an involved pattern, Zeros are sometimes used so that all sizes can be combined. For example, increase every sixth row 5{1-0} time(s) means the first size would increase 5 times, the second size would increase once, and the third size would do nothing.

MARKERS

As a convenience to you, we have used markers to help distinguish the beginning of a pattern. Place markers as instructed. You may use purchased markers or tie a length of contrasting color yarn around the needle. When you reach a marker on each row, slip it from the left needle to the right needle; remove it when no longer needed.

KNIT 2 TOGETHER *(abbreviated K2 tog)*

Insert the right needle into the **front** of the first two stitches on the left needle as if to **knit** *(Fig. 1)*, then **knit** them together as if they were one stitch.

Fig. 1

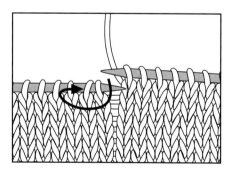

SLIP 1, KNIT 2 TOGETHER, PASS SLIPPED STITCH OVER
(abbreviated slip 1, K2 tog, PSSO)

Slip one stitch as if to **knit** *(Fig. 2a)*, then knit the next two stitches together *(Fig. 1)*. With the left needle, bring the slipped stitch over the stitch just made *(Fig. 2b)* and off the needle.

Fig. 2a

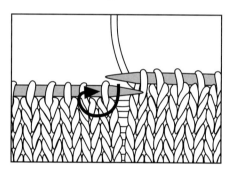

Fig. 2b

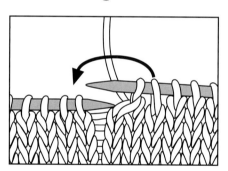

SLIP, SLIP, KNIT *(abbreviated SSK)*

Separately slip two stitches as if to **knit** *(Fig. 3a)*. Insert the **left** needle into the **front** of both slipped stitches *(Fig. 3b)* and then **knit** them together as if they were one stitch *(Fig. 3c)*.

Fig. 3a

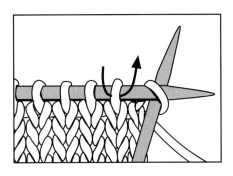

Fig. 3b

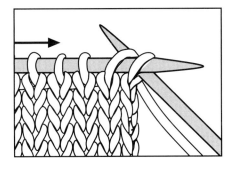

Fig. 3c

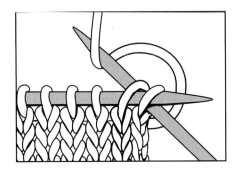

PURL 2 TOGETHER *(abbreviated P2 tog)*

Insert the right needle into the **front** of the first two stitches on the left needle as if to **purl** *(Fig. 4)*, then **purl** them together as if they were one stitch.

Fig. 4

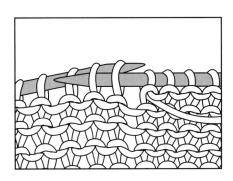

PURL 2 TOGETHER THROUGH THE BACK LOOP *(abbreviated P2 tog tbl)*

Insert the right needle into the **back** of both stitches from **back** to **front** *(Fig. 5)*, then **purl** them together as if they were one stitch.

Fig. 5

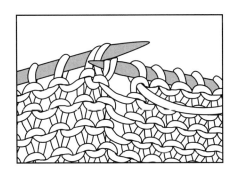

YARN OVERS

A yarn over *(abbreviated YO)* is simply placing the yarn over the right needle creating an extra stitch. Since the yarn over produces a hole in the knit fabric, it is used for a lacy effect. On the row following a yarn over, you must be careful to keep it on the needle and treat it as a stitch by knitting or purling it as instructed.

To make a yarn over, you'll loop the yarn over the needle like you would to knit or purl a stitch, bringing it either to the front or back of the piece so that it'll be ready to work the next stitch, creating a new stitch on the needle as follows:

After a knit stitch, before a knit stitch

Bring the yarn forward **between** the needles, then back **over** the top of the right hand needle, so that it is now in position to **knit** the next stitch *(Fig. 6a)*.

Fig. 6a

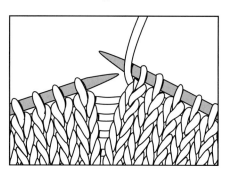

After a knit stitch, before a purl stitch

Bring the yarn forward **between** the needles, then back **over** the top of the right hand needle and forward **between** the needles again, so that it is now in position to **purl** the next stitch *(Fig. 6b)*.

Fig. 6b

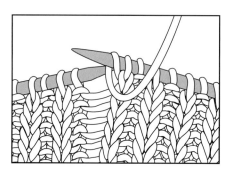

After a purl stitch, before a knit stitch

Take the yarn **over** the right hand needle to the back, so that it is now in position to **knit** the next stitch *(Fig. 6c)*.

Fig. 6c

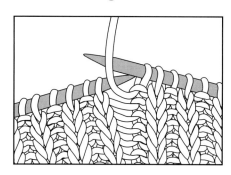

MAKE ONE *(abbreviated M1)*

Insert the **left** needle under the horizontal strand between the stitches from the **front** *(Fig. 7a)*. Then **knit** into the **back** of the strand *(Fig. 7b)*.

Fig. 7a

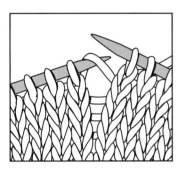

Fig. 7b

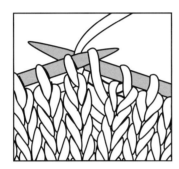

3-NEEDLE BIND OFF

Holding pieces with **right** sides together and needles parallel to each other, insert a third needle as if to **knit** into the first stitch on the front needle **and** into the first stitch on the back needle *(Fig. 8)*. Knit these two stitches together and slip them off the needle. ★ Knit the next stitch on each needle together and slip them off the needle. To bind off, insert the left needle into the first stitch on the right needle and pull the first stitch over the second stitch and off the right needle; repeat from ★ across until all of the stitches on the front needle have been bound off.

Fig. 8

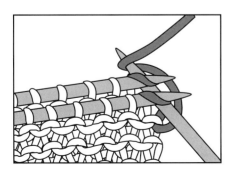

PICKING UP STITCHES

When instructed to pick up stitches, insert the needle from the **front** to the **back** under two strands at the edge of the worked piece *(Figs. 9a & b)*. Put the yarn around the needle as if to **knit**, then bring the needle with the yarn back through the stitch to the right side, resulting in a stitch on the needle.

Repeat this along the edge, picking up the required number of stitches.

A crochet hook may be helpful to pull yarn through.

Fig. 9a

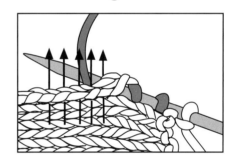

Fig. 9b

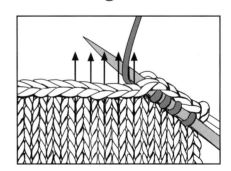

WEAVING SEAMS

With the **right** side of both pieces facing you and edges even, sew through both sides once to secure the seam. Insert the needle under the bar **between** the first and second stitches on the row and pull the yarn through **(Fig. 10)**. Insert the needle under the next bar on the second side. Repeat from side to side, being careful to match rows. If the edges are different lengths, it may be necessary to insert the needle under two bars at one edge.

Fig. 10

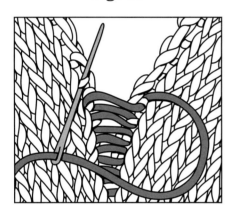

BASIC CROCHET STITCHES
CHAIN

To work a chain stitch, begin with a slip knot on the hook. Bring the yarn **over** hook from back to front, catching the yarn with the hook and turning the hook slightly toward you to keep the yarn from slipping off. Draw the yarn through the slip knot **(Fig. 11) (first chain st made, *abbreviated ch*)**.

Fig. 11

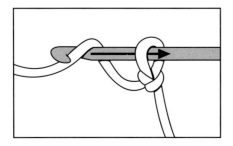

SLIP STITCH

To work a slip stitch, insert hook in stitch indicated, YO and draw through stitch and through loop on hook **(Fig. 12) (slip stitch made, *abbreviated slip st*)**.

Fig. 12

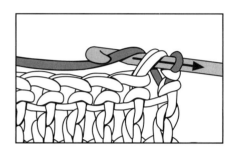

FINISH OFF

When you complete your last stitch, cut the yarn leaving a long end. Bring the loose end through the last loop on your hook and tighten it **(Fig. 13)**.

Fig. 13

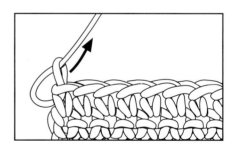

Yarn information

Each item in this leaflet was made using Light Weight Yarn. Any brand of Light Weight Yarn may be used. It is best to refer to the yardage/meters when determining how many balls or skeins to purchase. Remember, to arrive at the finished size, it is the GAUGE/TENSION that is important, not the brand of yarn.

For your convenience, listed below are colors used to create our photography models.

Blossom Baby Set
TLC® Baby
#5737 Powder Pink

Garland Baby Set
Red Heart® Soft Baby™
#7588 Lilac

Kitten Baby Set
Lion Brand® Baby Soft®
#106 Pastel Blue

For digital downloads of Leisure Arts' best-selling designs visit
www.leisureartslibrary.com

Production Team

Instructional Editor Joan Beebe

Editorial Writer Susan McManus Johnson

Graphic Artist Jeanne Zaffarano

Senior Graphic Artist Lora Puls

Photo Stylist Michelle Uhiren

Photographer Jason Masters